Grud

Sarah Power

T0284301

methuen | drama

LONDON · NEW YORK · OXFORD · NEW DELHI · SYDNEY

METHUEN DRAMA
Bloomsbury Publishing Plc
50 Bedford Square, London, WC1B 3DP, UK
1385 Broadway, New York, NY 10018, USA
29 Earlsfort Terrace, Dublin 2, Ireland

BLOOMSBURY, METHUEN DRAMA and the Methuen
Drama logo are trademarks of Bloomsbury Publishing Plc

First published in Great Britain 2024

Cover design: Rebecca Heselton

Cover image: Moon © Elena11/ Shutterstock. Armchair © GulArt/
Shutterstock. Balloon © Malenkka/ Shutterstock

A catalogue record for this book is available from the British Library.

Library of Congress Control Number: 2024938953.

ISBN: PB: 978-1-3505-0442-4
ePDF: 978-1-3505-0443-1
eBook: 978-1-3505-0444-8

Series: Modern Plays

Typeset by Mark Heslington Ltd, Scarborough, North Yorkshire
Printed and bound in Great Britain

To find out more about our authors and books visit
www.bloomsbury.com and sign up for our newsletters.

Grud was first performed at Hampstead Theatre Downstairs, London, on 28 June 2024. The cast was as follows:

BO	**Catherine Ashdown**
AICHA	**Kadiesha Belgrave**
GRUD	**Karl Theobald**

Writer	Sarah Power
Director	Jaz Woodcock-Stewart
Designer	Noemi Daboczi
Lighting Designer	Cheng Keng
Sound Designer	Cutty Sark
Co-Sound Designer	Jack Baxter

With big big thanks to

Tessa Walker.

Jessica Stewart.

Jaz Woodcock-Stewart. Catherine Ashdown, Kadiesha Belgrave and Karl Theobald. Noemi Daboczi. Adriana Perucca. Cheng Keng. Jack Baxter. James Dawson. Cutty Sark.

Greg and all the team at Hampstead Theatre.

Davina Moss. Chris Campbell.

Callan McCarthy.

My Hampstead Inspire crew: Jessica Norman, Magda Bird, Martha Watson Allpress, Mary Clapp, Nancy Netherwood, Nic McQuillan, Nicola May-Taylor, Sid Sagar, Patrick Swain, Dexter Flanders, Phoebe Frances Brown and Roy Williams.

My Dad, Mum and Laura for letting me write this and being nothing but supportive of it.

And Megan Glancy, Rebecca Nellis and Conrad Magan for cooking me so many dinners.

Grud

For my dad,
who I love.

Characters

Bo, *female, 17 years old*

Aicha, *female, 17 years old*

Grud, *male, late 40s / early 50s*

Notes on Staging

There are two places in this play – the flat and the college. As the play progresses the boundary between these two places should blur. They mess each other up.

The flat should feel dark and dangerous and disgusting. It should not feel like a home.

Grud *should always be present, sitting in the shadows of the other scenes.*

Scene One

Lights up on a sixth form college room.

Centre stage stands **Aicha**. *She is standing in front of a projector, keenly watching the door.*

Also on stage is a small scientific instrument.

Bo *enters. She is holding a printed timetable of college activities.*

Aicha   Helllooooo.

And welcome to SPACE.

On 'space' **Aicha** *presses 'on' on both a projector and a speaker, and a huge projection of the galaxy fills the room as music blares from the speaker. She's been rehearsing for this moment.*

Aicha *watches* **Bo**. **Bo** *looks up at the projection, then back at* **Aicha**.

There is a pause.

Aicha   It's like we're in space!

Pause.

Bo   It's very nice.

Aicha *looks at* **Bo** *again.*

Then she turns the projector and the music back off disgruntled.

Aicha   Are you not here for Space Club?

Bo   It said 'Physics Extended Project' on the timetable.

Pause.

I like 'Space Club' though. Sounds like a kid's TV show.

Bo *starts having a poke around Space Club.*

She finds the instrument.

What's this thing?

Aicha   Er, I'm not having a fascinating space chat with you after you've just mocked Space Club.

Bo *continues to look at the instrument.*

Aicha *watches her.*

Beat.

Aicha   I know you hey. You're the one that's always in the back of the library.

Like a little library gremlin.

Eating up knowledge.

Pause.

And Haribo.

Bo   I know you too, you ran for student president last year.

I remember your speech.

Aicha *is clearly embarrassed by this.*

Aicha   Student representative. This isn't America.

Beat.

And look, as I said afterwards in my statement, I wasn't trying to rip into the canteen staff, I was just trying to make a general point about not teaching people to settle for less in life.

But I wasn't trying to be a bitch about that pasta bake.

Although I do think it's heavily under-seasoned.

Bo   I liked your speech.

I thought it was very strong.

Aicha   Did you really?!

Thank you.

You know, I really appreciate you saying that because personally I felt I had really pulled it off and frankly I was a bit confused not to have won.

Beat.

So hang on, are you here for Space Club? Because don't take this the wrong way but you don't look very 'Space Club'.

Bo   Oh, well, I'm just sort of having a look at all the sessions.

Aicha   Oh right.

That's kind of weird.

Bo   Why?

Aicha   Do you have a general interest in all things?

Bo   Kind of I guess.

Well except geography.

Pause.

So is it just you in 'Space Club'?

Aicha   No.

They look at each other.

Bo   It is, isn't it.

Aicha   Just at the moment!

There was THREE of us last year.

But Ivan's orchestra got moved to a Thursday and Remi wanted to spend more time on his novel.

You know people have been slagging it but I actually think it has a lot of potential. It's about a dystopian future where everyone is a phone and they carry little people around in their pockets.

There is a pause.

(*Gesturing to the projector and speakers.*) Also I'm thinking after today like quite a lot more people are probably going to sign up.

Beat.

So, shall I explain the project? Because it's actually very interesting and amazing.

Bo   Yeah, go on.

Aicha   OK cool.

Well. Basically. We're helping Amir to design and make this instrument which is going to go to *space* to see if there are *aliens* living there.

No joke.

Bo   Who's Amir?

Aicha   PhD student.

Bo   And why does he hang out with you?

Aicha   It's like a scheme I think, like a 'help the kids' thing.

And I guess he gets to put it on his CV. And being real, we're here to put it on our UCAS, so everyone's playing the same game at the end of the day.

Poor guy though, I think he was hoping all these gang members would turn up and he would inspire them away from knife crime by teaching them about gravity.

But then obviously it was just three geeks.

Bo   Actual aliens?

Aicha   Well.

The instrument is looking for water. If it finds it, that means organisms *could* live on the planet.

Bo   What type of organisms?

Aicha   Like little creatures.

Beat – **Bo** *is looking at* **Aicha** *quite intently.*

Bo   How big are the little creatures?

Pause.

Aicha   They count as creatures.

Bo   How big are they?

Beat.

Aicha   Like one cell.

Bo *gives* **Aicha** *a 'that's not an alien' look.*

Aicha   It's very exciting OK!

Bo   Sure.

Well, thank you for the introduction to the project.

Bo *makes to leave.*

Aicha   Hey hey!

Bo   What?

Beat.

Aicha   Come back next week like.

Bo   Maybe.

Depends what chemistry club are saying, doesn't it.

Scene Two

The flat.

A dishevelled man is lying in the middle of the dirty floor, passed out, surrounded by a few beer cans and food wrappers. This is **Grud**.

The sound of bad TV plays.

We can hear **Bo** *entering.*

Grud *starts as she enters. Without getting up he makes a poor attempt to hide some of the rubbish gathered around him, then his head falls back down.*

Bo *walks further into the flat.* **Grud** *awakens again and looks around at her.*

He tries to do some small talk, but he's too far gone.

Grud (*slurred*)   Heelll . . . Hel . . . squ . . . hel . . .

. . . School . . .

?

Bo *looks at him and doesn't say anything.*

Grud *grimaces – he can tell he's fucking up.*

Bo *moves past him, as she does so* **Grud** *grabs her ankle – it's meant to be playful but he's too drunk to judge it right.*

Grud *giggles.*

Bo   Get off.

Grud   . . . got your . . .

Ankle!

Grud *wobbles* **Bo**'s *ankle,* **Bo** *trips back slightly.*

Bo   Don't.

Grud   Ankle ankle ankle ankle ankle!

Bo   Seriously, stop!

So annoying, man.

Grud *is trying to wobble* **Bo**'s *leg again as* **Bo** *gently tries to kick him off.*

Suddenly **Grud** *starts to gag from the motion of it all and he lets go.*

It seems like he's going to be sick.

She looks at him, worried and disgusted.

Bo   You alright?

His retching stops.

He looks at her, embarrassed.

Scene Three

Aicha *and* **Bo** *are at Space Club.*

Aicha   Billy said he didn't really know you except that you're in his maths set.

Bo   Yeah.

Aicha   You're so elusive. How do you not know anyone?

Bo   I do know people.

Aicha   Not outside of class tho.

What do you do for lunch?

Bo   Depends.

Aicha   What did you do last lunch?

Bo   Why does it matter.

Aicha   Do you never sit in the hall?

Bo   Not normally.

Aicha   Do you go park?

Bo   Sometimes.

Aicha   It's just weird 'cause it's like, you aren't that weird or anything.

Like if you wanted to you could.

But you've chosen to be a Billy no mates.

Beat.

That's an ironic name for Billy now I think about it.

He's like outrageously popular.

So are you dating anyone at the moment?

Bo   No . . .

Aicha   Yeah, me neither.

Just my studies. Lol.

I'm joking. I'm not actually dating my studies.

I would actually LOVE to be dating someone to be honest but I'm not looking at like, maximum options over here.

I actually asked Billy's mate out recently you know, Elliot Park.

I thought we had a vibe.

Beat.

He said we didn't.

Beat.

Shit man, I like your little pencil set.

You're so cute, aren't you. With all your little things.

And your little binder with the little dividers and everything.

'Organised and ready to learn.'

Aicha *is touching* **Bo***'s things, it's making* **Bo** *tense.*

Bo   Can you not.

Bo *moves the stuff away from* **Aicha***.*

She sorts it out slightly.

Puts it away.

Aicha *watches her, bemused.*

Aicha   OK. So do you want to meet him?

Bo   Who?

Aicha *picks up the scientific instrument.*

Aicha   Kerbal!

Kerbal the CubeSat!

Well.

Technically the model of a CubeSat.

Bo   Wait, what?

Aicha   What?

Bo   Model? Are you kidding?

Aicha   What?

Bo   So this isn't even going to space?

Aicha   Yeah, it is, it is . . .

Beat.

Just not *this* one.

Beat.

A Kerbal is going into space.

And our Kerbal is a very accurate model of that Kerbal.

But made from more affordable materials.

Beat.

We're doing an extended project, Bo! We're obviously not designing something which is actually going to space.

Like, come on.

Bo   This project, man.

Aicha   Err, you won't be saying that when they tell us we can go watch the launch.

Bo   Did they say that?

Aicha   Yeah.

Said they might be able to fund it off the scheme and we can go Manchester and see him off.

Like real Kerbal, not our Kerbal.

Bo   That would be fun.

Aicha   I know, would be sick.

I'm quite hyped.

Bo   Where is Amir anyway?

Aicha   Probably not coming.

He's a bit of a wasteman, truth be told.

Beat.

Aicha   You know who did say they knew you.

Georgia.

Said she knows you from Primary.

Said you're a psycho and that she knows about you and the ferret.

Bo *visibly reacts to this.*

Aicha   Wouldn't tell me what happened tho.

Quite *intriguing*.

Aicha *is staring at* **Bo** *in mock interrogation.*

Beat.

Aicha   Did you kill it?

Eat it?

Make love to it?

Bo *pauses for a moment. Then . . .*

Bo   None of the above.

Scene Four

In the flat.

Grud *sits listening to Blues Run the Game – Simon and Garfunkel. He's drinking a can. He's pretty drunk.*

He listens to the intro, then as the song has only just begun, he starts it over again.

He listens to the intro again – then again after the intro, starts it back to the beginning.

He does it again.

We watch **Bo** *standing for a moment outside, listening.*

Then she enters.

Grud *turns off his music hastily.*

Grud (*slurred*)   Hellooooo championnnnn!

Bo the championnnnn

The championnn!

Bo   Hello.

Bo *moves into the space – she starts to tidy it up a bit,* **Grud** *realises what's she's doing and feels a bit guilty.*

Grud   No no don't, I'll do THAT I'll do THATTTT later.

Was planning to do it later.

Had a BIG plan (*Tapping side of his head.*) to do . . .

That . . .

He's already forgotten what it was he's talking about.

Later . . .

Bo *ignores him.*

Grud (*light*)   Did you have a . . . fun day?

Bo   Yeah, it was alright.

Did you go to work?

Grud   Yes.

There is a pause.

No.

Bo *looks at him.*

Grud   Yes.

Beat.

For a little bit.

Bo *looks at him.*

Grud   Had drinks with the new kid.

Mark . . .?

Matthew . . .?

He's remembered:

Barney.

He zones out, then back in.

Went to the cinema!

Bo (*surprised*)   You went to the cinema?

Grud   Yes!

Bo   What did you see?

Grud   That new . . . Marvel film.

Pause.

Bo   I don't think that's out yet.

Grud   Oh . . . yes.

No . . .

Beat.

(*Quite a sudden shift in tone.*) Needed to take out the new kid because Tony was being a DICK CUNT.

Needed to help Brenden, show him . . . not everyone is such CUNTS.

Beat – **Bo** *is already bored.*

Bo   Uhuh.

Grud   He's saying . . . he's fucking saying . . .

Getting wound up, shaking his head.

Giving me this little 'chat' little timesheets little 'can you do this' . . . To ME *me* saying *I'm* late . . . on . . .

. . . stupid little brain wouldn't even understand, his stupid little (*Tapping his head.*) not technical. Untrained. UNEDUCATED . . .

Bo *is finding this boring and annoying.*

Bo   I don't think you should say 'uneducated' like that /

He doesn't acknowledge he's heard this.

Grud   / Patronising *bullshit.*

So I think . . . I'm not . . . TAKING THIS . . .

Bullshit.

So I left.

Take Barney.

For protection.

Take him to the pub.

And that was good because he was upset, but *I* managed to calm him down and he said by the end of our chat he was feeling . . . MUCH better and *I* said to pay no notice of DICK CUNT FUCKING TONY don't worry Brendan DON'T WORRY, don't worry don't worry . . . I remember, I remember being young SCARED but it's . . . it's OK! You can one day you'll be one day senior and you'll see a lot of *Tonys* have seen a LOT of TONYS in your time and you'll know how to handle a *Tony.*

Beat – **Grud** *is looking to* **Bo** *for a response, she's not looking as impressed as he'd like.*

Grud   And I know how to handle a Tony.

I know.

Because before we went for drinks . . .

In the car park I see his car . . .

See his stupid flashy car.

Untechnical make-up-for-it-with-my-shit-car car . . .

and I think . . .

I know.

Beat.

And I get out my key, and I do a little scrape all down the side.

Grud *giggles.*

Bo   Whoahhhh what?!

Grud   That'll show him.

Show him not to be like that. Little cunt so he is.

Grud *genuinely thinks this was a good idea.*

Bo   You keyed his car?!

Grud   What?

Bo's *reaction makes* **Grud** *realise maybe this wasn't a good idea after all.*

Grud   No . . . no no no . . . just joking.

. . . Joking.

Beat – **Bo** *is staring at him.*

Grud   Nooo Bo, why are you always so serious.

I didn't . . . I didn't *key his car.*

Beat.

Well, not too much anyway . . .

He smiles at her in a 'only messing' way.

Joking! JOKINGGGGGGG.

Pause – **Bo** *is watching him.*

She decides to leave it.

Bo   Did you get any food?

Grud   Yes.

Bo   If you're lying I am going to find out in one second when I look in the fridge /

Grud   / I did! Go look, it's a surprise!

Bo *moves to the kitchen, she opens the fridge – inside is nothing but piles and piles of Monster Munch crisps.*

Bo   You got crisps.

Grud   I got your *favourite* crisps.

LOTS of them.

LOTS AND LOTS AND LOTS OF THEM.

For a TREAT.

There is a pause – **Grud** *is pleased with himself. After a moment he falls back into semi-consciousness.*

Bo *looks at the crisps again, annoyed, but maybe also a tiny part of her seeing the humour in it.*

She takes a packet out.

She opens them and sits for a moment next to **Grud***, who remains in his drunken half sleep.*

Beat.

Bo   Was Tony having the little chat with you or with Barney?

Grud   Wha?

Bo   You said Tony had a little chat with you?

Grud   Yes.

Had our one . . . two . . . one . . . two . . .

Pause.

Bo   So you took Barney out because Tony had a go at *you*?

Grud (*not seeing the problem*)   Yes.

Bo   Right.

Beat.

Were you late?

Grud   Wha?

Bo   Like what Tony said, did it happen?

Grud (*big lies*)   No no no . . .

No.

Beat.

Bo   You can't just do whatever you want you know.

Even if you are 'very technical'.

Grud   –

Pause.

Bo   Give us your wallet then.

Grud *gives* **Bo** *his wallet.*

Bo *gets up, she picks up her bag and goes out to get some shopping.*

Scene Five

Space Club.

Bo *and* **Aicha** *are waiting.*

Aicha   Oh shit, I am EXCITED.

Bo   We don't know if we're going yet.

Aicha   Aaaaaaahhhhhhhhhhhhhhhhhhhhhhhh

Oh my god.

Tense, isn't it?

Bo   I feel like you're making it tenser.

Aicha   Aaaaaaaa /

Bo *looks at* **Aicha**.

Aicha *stops*.

Pause.

Aicha   If we get to go are you gonna cry?

Bo   To Manchester?

Aicha   It's a big moment!

Pause – **Aicha** *starts fidgeting with something.*

Aicha   Did you get your mock results back?

Bo   Yeah.

Aicha   And?

Beat.

Bo   I got 100 per cent.

Aicha   Fuck off. In physics?

Bo   In all of them.

Aicha *stops moving.*

Aicha   Are you serious?

Bo   Yeah.

Aicha   Oh my god.

Beat.

Are you a psychopath?

Bo   Why would that help?

Aicha   I don't know.

They just have that vibe, don't they.

Christ.

Fucking hell, Bo, that's insane.

Seriously, that is amazing. Well done.

Bo   Thanks.

How were yours?

Aicha   I got three A stars too, obvs.

Space Club legendssssss.

Bo   I wish you wouldn't call it that.

Aicha *smiles.*

Beat.

Aicha   Are you hyped for uni then?

Bo   Yeah.

Aicha   Yeah, me too.

Just hope I get into King's or my mum will actually kill me.

Beat.

What are your parents like? Are they chill or not really?

Bo *lies about her parents completely flawlessly. If we didn't know, we wouldn't know.*

Bo   Same I guess really.

Aicha *looks at her watch.*

Aicha   Oh my god, it's time.

You know what, fuck it, I'm just going in. They can finish their meeting afterwards.

Aicha *gets up and starts to walk confidently into the meeting room.*

Bo *follows after her.*

Bo   Aicha, you can't just go in!

Aicha   I am literally doing it right this moment actually, mate, soooo.

They disappear off.

The lights remain on in the college.

We watch the empty room and the shadows.

We can hear movement from the flat. We can see **Grud** *moving about, but we can't really see what he's doing.*

A pause.

Then suddenly **Aicha** *bursts out of the meeting room.*

Bo *follows behind her.*

Aicha   OH.

MY.

GOD.

Aicha *starts running around the room.*

Aicha   Yayayayayayayayayayayayayayayayayayayayayayayayayaya yayayayayay!

Aicha *jumps on a chair or a table.*

Yayayayayayayayayayayayayayayayayayayayayayayayayayayayaya yay!

She does the next bit to a dance.

Yes yes yes yes YES.

Then she notices **Bo**.

Aicha   Aren't you excited?

Bo   Yeah, for sure.

It's really exciting.

Aicha *is looking disappointed, she gets down from the chair a bit embarrassed.*

Bo   I really am. Honest.

I just can't . . .

But I really am.

Pause.

Aicha   Oh my god, do you think we'll get a hotel room?

Bo   I think we'll probs just do it in a day /

Aicha   / And a hotel breakfast!

Bo   I think it's like two hours /

Aicha   / And we'll get drunk in the hotel bar in the evening

Bo   Aicha /

Aicha   / And maybe have like a confusing romantic moment cause we're so overwhelmed by it all.

Bo   Really don't see that happening.

Aicha (*mock offended*)   Wow.

They smile at each other.

Then quite quickly **Aicha** *makes to hug* **Bo**.

Bo *flinches away from her, instinctively.*

Aicha *stops.*

They look at each other.

Aicha *goes to hug* **Bo** *again, slower this time.*

Bo *hugs her back.*

There is a pause.

Then **Bo** *realises something has started to leak into the college from the flat.*

A liquid is spreading across the floor.

She's looking at it, horrified.

Aicha *can't see it. She moves back.*

Bo   Hey, don't.

Aicha   What?

Bo *moves out of the college and into the flat.*

Bo   Don't step there.

Scene Six

In the flat.

Grud *is cleaning up a spilt drink – the drink which has spilt into the college.*

We watch **Grud** *for a while – tidying the flat. His movement is completely different to anything which has come before. He isn't swaying around, his speech in this scene is normal – he's sober.*

He notices a stain on his shirt.

Grud   Ah fuck.

He takes his shirt off, throws it in the washing.

There is bad bruising all down one side of his body. He doesn't seem too shocked by this, but a bit confused – he inspects it for a moment.

He lifts his arm above his head, it hurts.

Bo *enters, he doesn't realise, she catches a glimpse of the bruising as* **Grud** *is finding a cleaner shirt and putting it on.*

He smooths his new shirt out a bit.

She stands watching him for a second.

Grud *notices her.*

Grud   Spilt something on me shirt, what am I like, hey?

Bo *makes a vague gesture of acknowledgement.*

Grud   How was college, you hanging in there?

Bo   It's alright, yeah.

Grud   You must of gone down to the canal after class for a bit, did you?

Bo   For a bit, yeah.

Beat.

Grud   MasterChef's on if you fancy it.

It's been inspiring me, I'm going to try and do fondant potatoes with all those old spuds we need to get through.

Bo *is watching him very closely.*

Grud   How does that sound?

Bo   Yeah.

Sounds good.

There's a pause.

They stare at each other for a moment – then she goes for it.

Bo   I got my mock results back.

Grud   Did you?

Bo   Yeah.

Beat.

I got all A stars.

Grud   You did?!

Bo   Yeah.

Grud *looks like he's about to cry.*

Grud   Oh bloody hell, Bo! Oh bloody hell, you're. God. You're a bloody superstar!

Well done.

Bo *smiles.*

Grud *holds his arms out awkwardly.*

Grud   Ahh go on, give us a hug.

They hug. It's a bit awkward but full of love.

Grud (*doing an impression*)   It's just FANTASTIC, *REALLY*, you can just really TASTE that strong foundation in the sciences coming through, mixing with the *earthiness* of a well-structured essay, and just a *hint* of well-formulated mathematical reasoning.

Bo *laughs.*

Grud   That was Greg Wallace eating your results.

Bo   Yeah, I got it.

Grud *beams.*

Grud   Ah Christ.

There is a pained look on his face for a moment, then a smile.

Then suddenly mock serious.

Alright then superstar, come on now, you sit down here, this is a good time for me to give you some important life advice.

You ready?

There is a joke coming – **Bo** *can see this and is ready to get involved.*

Bo *nods also mock serious.*

OK. So. First things first.

Never punch a lizard.

Bo *nods.*

Grud   It's mean. They don't like it. It's never the solution.

Bo   Sure.

Grud   OK, good. Secondly.

ALWAYS wear a hat.

Bo   You aren't wearing a hat right now.

Grud   I know, and look what happened to me!

Bo *laughs despite herself.*

Grud *laughs too.*

Grud   OK, and finally, you want to know the MOST important piece of advice?

Bo   Yeah, go on.

Grud   The biggest most *important* thing you can never ever forget to do.

Bo   Yeah.

Grud   OK.

THIRDLY.

Always . . .

We think maybe something serious is coming for a moment, but then . . .

carry an earwig.

Bo   Always carry an earwig?

Grud   Somewhere about your person, yes.

For emergencies.

Bo   Sure. So somewhere accessible?

Somewhere like:

She makes a quick motion miming retrieving an earwig like a cowboy retrieves a gun.

BAM

Earwig.

Grud *laughs.*

Grud   Exactly.

BAM.

Earwig.

They have an earwig shooting match . . .

Bo   Bam.

Earwig /

Grud   / Bam.

Earwig.

They laugh – a cute moment passes between them.

Beat.

Grud   Was thinking we should go on a nice HOLIDAY soon, don't you think, squelch? We could go on a trip to the Amazon! I've always wanted to go to the Amazon, Heart of Darkness, into the unknown, the depth of the earth, the future and past of humanity! Sort out the meaning of life once and for all.

Get it done.

What do you reckon?

Bo   Yeah, sounds good.

Grud   We went on some nice holidays when you were little, you know. Took you all round Ireland in that old backpack thing. Got so worried about you being cold we got you this massive puffer jacket and you were so little and the coat was so huge – you were completely spherical. With your little round head on top and these two little hands poking out each side.

Puffer fish, that's what we called you.

He laughs.

That was a good laugh that trip.

Pause.

Bo   Did you hurt your side?

Grud   Nah, it's nothing.

Pause.

Bo   What happened?

Grud   Must of fallen.

Don't actually . . .

Don't remember.

Pause.

Bo   Was it . . . do you think it was a fight?

Grud   No, just a fall, I think.

(*Awkward.*) I'd remember a fight . . .

Beat.

Bo   Do you think you should go to the doctor?

Grud   It's fine.

Beat.

Bo   OK.

Beat.

Do you think you should go to the doctor for . . .

Grud   For what?

It's awkward – they both know what she's referring to.

She can't say it.

Grud   I don't need to see a doctor.

I'm fine.

Beat.

I was going to say . . . I might go on a bit of a health kick for a while anyway!

At my age, got to start doing those kinds of things, you know.

Eat the rainbow.

Run a marathon.

Save a baby from a burning building.

Have a few less . . .

Beat.

You know, just sort it all out a bit.

Beat.

Bo   OK, yeah. Sounds good.

Pause.

Grud   You still kicking around with that Ruby kid?

Bo   Ruby? That was like ten years ago.

Grud   Ah right.

Yeah, of course . . .

Beat.

Bo   There's this girl at college I've been hanging out with a bit tho.

We're doing this project together.

Grud   Ah yeah?! What's her name?

Bo   Aicha.

Grud   Aicha. What's she like then?

Bo *smiles*.

Bo   She's funny.

Grud   All the best people are.

Well, she must be doing something right if you like her.

Pause.

Come on, then! Let's watch this bloody show shall we!

Better make the most of it, we won't be able to do this soon enough.

Scene Seven

Space Club.

Aicha *bursts in*.

Aicha   I think there's a fight happening outside!

Bo   Really?

Aicha   Yeah!

Bo   Who?

Aicha   Tiago and that hat boy.

Bo   What hat boy?

Aicha   Hat boy!

Bo   Ohhhh yeah, him.

Aicha   Shall we go?

Bo   What?

Aicha   Watch it, man! It's a fight!

Bo   What? No.

Aicha   Come onnnn, Bo, please!

Bo   No.

Aicha   Everyone is down there. I think it's really gonna pop off!

Hat boy's called his mate from the BTEC college and Tiago called his mate from home and I think it's gonna get mental and /

Bo   / I'm not going to go watch some tragic little fight between two loser twat virgins who think they're hard trying to impress a girl whose greatest achievement in life is having a tattoo very close to her clit.

Aicha   Wowwwwww OK.

Awkward pause.

Bo   What?

Aicha   I dunno, man.

You don't have to hate on everyone the whole time, you know.

There is an awkward pause.

Bo   They're cunts.

Aicha   I think they're alright.

*Beat – this has got to **Bo**.*

Aicha *tries to make peace a bit.*

Aicha   I think you're just jealous 'cause you want in the fight.

Probably reckon you could scare them to death with your ability to do mental arithmetic really really fast.

Beat.

How's Kerbs?

Bo   Fiddly.

Aicha (*mock voice*)   'Fiddly.'

Let me see, then.

Aicha *moves towards* **Bo**. **Bo** *immediately backs away slightly.*

Aicha *looks pissed off and a bit hurt.*

Aicha   Why do you always do that?

Bo   Do what?

Pause.

Aicha   Move away from me like that.

Bo   I don't.

Aicha   You do.

The moment I get near you, you back off like I'm some gross thing.

Beat.

Bo   It's not like that.

*Pause – **Aicha** is looking hurt.*

Bo *is looking at* **Aicha**.

Bo   Aicha.

Come on, man.

It's not like that . . .

Bo *hesitates.*

Then she goes for it.

Do I smell weird?

Beat.

Aicha   What?

Bo   When you get near to me . . . do I . . .

. . . smell bad to you?

Beat.

Aicha *has understood.*

Aicha   No.

No, you don't smell bad.

Bo   OK.

Beat.

Thanks.

They get back to Kerbal.

There is a pause.

Bo   I don't hate on everyone the whole time.

Aicha   I know.

Long pause as they work.

Bo   Do you ever worry you're a bad person?

Aicha   What?

Bo   Like, do you ever worry you might do something really bad.

Pause.

Aicha   Like what?

Bo   I don't know. Just like, something bad.

Aicha   I don't understand.

Bo   Doesn't matter.

Beat.

*Then **Bo** finally gets something working – Kerbal lights up or makes a noise.*

Bo   Ah yeah.

Aicha   Oh shit, nice one!

(*To Kerbal.*) Look at YOU, Special K!

Aicha *holds Kerbal and stares at him with deep love and affection.*

We should test him.

Without a second thought **Aicha** *throws Kerbal directly into the floor.*

Bo   What the fuck!

Bo *looks down at him then back up at* **Aicha**, *perplexed.*

Aicha   What?

He has to be robust.

Bo *stares at her.*

Aicha   He's going to space, Bo.

He needs to be strong.

Ready for lift off!

Aicha *picks him up.*

Aicha   And look!

He's fine, the little trooper.

Pause – they both stare at him.

Bo   He's so tiny.

Aicha   A tiny little CubeSat who is going to change everything.

Beat.

Then suddenly and without warning there is a huge roar from the flat.

Bo *looks up, panicked.*

Scene Eight

Music blasts from the flat.

Grud *is dancing and hanging up decorations, slurping from a little glass of prosecco as he does so.*

Everything feels chaotic and unstable.

Bo *enters.*

Grud   Booooooooooooo!!!

She's homeeeeeeeeee SHE'S
HOMEEEEEEEEEEEEEEEEEEE

He goes to hug her, it's clumsy and a little rough.

Bo   Hello.

Beat.

What are you doing?

Grud   Getting READY.

For our CELEBRATION!

Bo   What for?

Grud   For you the championnnnn the
CHAMPIONNNNN

BO THE CHAMPIONNNNNNNN

I am sooooooo proud of YOU

So prouddddd

SO Proud, so so proud, so so so so so so proud. So so so so so
so so PROUDDDDD.

Bo   Thank you.

She's anxious.

Grud   I cooked!

She's genuinely super surprised.

Bo   What?

Grud   Yes, that's RIGHT!

YES.

Bo   What did you cook?

Grud *reveals a bag from the chippy.*

Grud   Fish 'n' chips!

Bo *laughs despite herself.*

Bo   Very good.

Grud *beams, he's so delighted the joke has gone down well he's going to try another.*

Grud   Bo Bo Bo, guess what!

Bo   What?

Grud   Earlier. When you were out. A GIRAFFE. Was here.

Bo   Er . . .

Grud   Yes. A giraffe. Was here. Knocking for you! /

She's understood.

Bo   / Oh yeah.

Grud   Yes. At the back door. Looking for you.

But I guess you / miss it.

Bo   / missed it.

Yeah.

She smiles at him. This is an old joke which they both know well.

Grud   Ah, but you are too old now!

Too old for my silly jokes.

Grud *beams at* **Bo**.

Bo *senses something isn't right.*

Bo   How was work?

Long pause.

How was work?

Grud   Ugh. STUPID. Let's not talk about WORK. Stupid good-for-nothing WORK.

Beat – **Bo** *is looking at him expectantly.*

Grud   Barney complained.

Bo   What did he say?

Grud   *Tony* said. *Tony* said he said.

He probably didn't probably not probably not true bullshit.

Tony twisting things.

Beat – they look at each other.

Said I was . . .

Messy.

Unprofessional.

'Unprofessional.'

I didn't do anything! Took the lad for a couple of drinks.

Trying to be nice. Trying to help. Friendly. Hard starting in that place.

Scared little graduate, I remember, being young, scared.

Took him to the BFI bar.

Nice there. Got a few beers.

'Unprofessional.'

Fucking Tony fucking cunting little shit.

Beat.

Bo   How many /

Grud   / Put me on a probation period.

Like I'm the fucking young lad.

Ridiculous.

Bo   Have you . . .

Are you going to lose your job?

Grud   What?! No! No of course not!

Lost my job!

Just this stupid . . . process . . . Tony . . . Tony talking shit, LOVES process.

Idiot.

Bo (*she's pissed off*)   / Tony is your boss.

Grud   / Stupid fucking idiot twat, so he is.

BUT. BUT BUT BUT BUT.

That's not what we're all about right now!

Because right now we're CELEBRATING!

Celebrating, SQUELCH.

Then he goes over to get the second bottle of prosecco and a bottle of vodka.

He clumsily pours out two glasses of vodka and prosecco.

He passes one to **Bo**.

Grud   Cocktails!

Bo   Let's not have cocktails.

Grud   But we're celebrating!

Bo   Yeah, I know, but let's just . . . I don't want, I have to study.

Let's just have the chips and that.

Grud   No no no no no no no no no no no no no no!

I got it for you!

Grud *downs his drink. Then he pours himself another.*

For celebrating our little squelch!

Grud *downs the next drink. He pours himself another.*

He drinks that. He pours another.

He drinks that. He pours another.

Bo *is watching him.*

He looks up at her.

Suddenly there is a shift in mood – she's angry.

Bo   What are we celebrating?

Beat.

Grud   You!

Bo   What about me?

Grud   Your ACHIEVEMENTS!

Beat.

Bo   Which achievements?

Grud   Your ones.

Beat.

Bo   Yeah, but what did I achieve?

A horrible pause.

Grud   Your . . .

He's fighting to remember.

Your studies.

Bo   What studies?

Grud *is getting upset, under his drunken haze he's fighting to keep hold of facts.*

Grud   It's your studies, we're celebrating your studies.

You did well in your studies.

So we are celebrating and I have done . . .

NICE THINGS

For YOU.

He is getting angry.

And you come in here and you, you, youuuuuuuu come in here and you /

Bo   / What studies?

Grud   University.

Bo   I'm not at uni.

Grud (*growls*)   Yes. Not uni. I know it's not uni.

Bo   But you said /

Grud   / Going to uni. FOR UNI. Studies FOR uni.

Listen.

Listen listen HERE listen because I am just trying to do NICE THINGS. Nice things for you for YOU!

And you try to fuck with

Fuck with me fuck over fuck me fuck

With ME

He's becoming animalistic, pacing around.

And I know about you.

Don't you patronise me. I know about YOU so don't say I don't know I know I know about

Selfish. So SELFISH

He starts ripping all of the decorations down.

All these NICE THINGS

He finishes his drink and pours another.

All these NICE THINGS FOR YOU

He finishes his drink and pours another.

Things I NEVER GOT

Things which NEVER HAPPENED TO ME

NICE THINGS ALL THE TIME FOR YOU ALL THE FUCKING TIME

And I look after YOU pay for YOU food for YOU for me? Did I get that? NO NEVER NEVER NEVER NEVER but for you? YOU ALL THE FUCKING TIME ALL THESE THINGS.

THINGS THINGS THINGS

He finishes his drink and pours another.

And you are UNGRATEFUL.

SO UNGRATEFUL.

Grud *picks up a chair and starts smashing it into the floor again and again and again.*

He is now frantic and upset and completely out of control. It is terrifying.

Bo *stands, paralysed by it.*

Grud   SELFISH.

SPOILT.

NICE THINGS.

Grud *is smashing and smashing.*

Bo *goes to move towards him and then seems to think better of it.*

He starts to move over towards **Bo**.

Bo   Don't.

She's suddenly frightened.

He is seeming more and more panicked, he's trapping **Bo***, cornering her.*

Bo   Grud, come on.

Don't.

He is howling, it's scary and intimidating. There is so much rage.

Then we start to realise.

He's sad.

He's desperately sad.

He collapses onto her, crying and gross.

They collapse to the floor together.

There is quiet for a long time.

Then **Grud** *suddenly switches.*

Grud   Bo!

He turns to her – he has entirely forgotten what has come before.

Bo!

Bo   What?

Grud   Earlier. Earlier. When you were out. A hedgehog. A HEDGEHOG was here. Knocking at the door. For YOU.

Beat – he's staring at her in mock surprise.

Bo *looks at him.*

Bo   Crazy.

I guess I must of / missed it.

Grud   / Missed it!

Grud *laughs, so happy the joke has worked.*

Bo *remains sitting with* **Grud** *as* **Aicha** *begins her scene.*

Scene Nine

Space Club.

Aicha   Will you come to Georgia's party with me on Saturday?

Bo *speaks her lines whilst still sitting in the previous scene.*

Bo   I don't like Georgia.

Aicha   Yeah, but everyone is going. It's not like you'll even talk to her.

Please, Bo. You never come to things with me.

Bo   I just don't know if I can.

Bo *moves fully into the scene and the flat fades away slightly, but we continue to feel* **Grud***'s presence more than before.*

Aicha   Why?

Bo   Busy.

Aicha   With what?

Bo   Stuff.

There is a tense pause.

Aicha   Fine. Whatever. I don't really care.

Would just be nice to go with someone for once.

I'm sick of always going to things on my ones.

Bo   Billy and that will be there.

Aicha   They aren't my mates tho, are they.

Being real about it.

Like they think I'm alright.

But nobody is my actual mate.

Beat.

They look at each other, both realising the extent of the friendship for the first time.

Aicha *needs her.*

This panics **Bo** *on some level she's not fully aware of.*

Aicha   Would just be nice if some people actually thought I was alright. I know you don't care but I do actually think that's important sometimes.

'Human connection' and that, you know.

Beat.

And Elliot is going.

AND I got a party jacket which I was gonna wear which looks really good.

AND I got us some beers.

AND I asked Billy if you could come with and he said it was cool.

AND /

Bo   / I'm not fucking going with you, Aicha!

And I can't make people like you if nobody does.

You'd have to be less of a weird little geek for that.

Beat.

It has come out way too harsh.

Aicha *is completely thrown.*

She suddenly seems quiet, embarrassed, awkward.

All her front and power is gone.

We have never seen her like this before.

Bo *is immediately horrified at herself.*

They stand looking at each other.

Then **Aicha** *picks up her stuff.*

Lights up on **Grud** *as he begins his scene in the flat – both scenes run parallel over the next lines.*

Aicha   You want to know why you didn't get invited, Bo?

Because you're mean to people.

And that's worse.

Aicha *leaves.*

Bo *stands, stunned at herself and horrified.*

Scene Ten

The flat.

Grud *sits in his chair. The TV is on gently.*

He is falling asleep, his eyes keep closing slightly, then opening, then closed.

He's asleep.

We watch him for a while.

His face starts to pain.

He's having a nightmare.

It's getting worse.

His body is starting to move in strange ways, he's trying to get away from something we can't see, something he's very afraid of.

He's moaning and making strange noises.

Then he screams. It's horrible and full of fear.

Then suddenly his eyes are wide open.

He bolts out of the chair, he's standing, breathing heavily, crying.

He's pure panic, the panic of a child.

He's seeing things which aren't there around him. He is making the same movements he made in the dream. He's seeing the same images.

Then he realises they aren't there. He's in the flat.

He starts to move around the flat, he turns on every light in turn until they are piercingly bright.

Then he moves to the TV and turns it up higher and higher and higher until it's deafening.

Then he turns the radio on and turns it up and up and up.

Then he gets a bottle of whiskey and a glass.

He fills the glass, shaking.

He looks at it for a moment.

Then he moves to the kitchen and pours it away.

He moves back to his chair.

After a moment he pours another glass.

He moves to the kitchen.

He looks like he's going to pour it away again but then quite suddenly he downs it.

Standing and crying and still half in the panic attack he fills another glass and downs it.

And another.

And another.

He's becoming calmer in his body, but he's still crying, ashamed of what he's doing.

But the panic is subsiding. The drink is helping.

After a moment he slowly starts to move back over to sit back in his chair.

He is safe now. Surrounded by his lights and his noise and his drink.

He lets himself calm, but there is still so much shame in it.

He doesn't close his eyes, he doesn't dare.

He watches the TV.

He looks sad and small and alone.

Scene Eleven

Bo *is moving towards the flat.*

She sees all the lights on, she hears the TV.

She stands outside, listening.

Then she turns around.

She moves away off towards the canal.

She finds somewhere to sit.

She takes off her shoes and socks and puts her feet in the water.

It's cold.

Then her feet start to numb. It's nice.

She takes out a packet of crisps.

She opens her crisps and eats one.

She sits, waiting.

She looks sad and small and alone.

Scene Twelve

Space Club.

Bo   I'm sorry.

I was being a cunt.

I don't know why I did that, I didn't mean it.

Like at all.

They look at each other.

Aicha *looks unsure.*

Bo   I think you're so excellent.

I think everything about you is how a person should be.

There is a long pause.

Aicha   Yeah, you were a cunt actually.

Bo   I know.

Aicha   Don't ever speak to me like that again, OK?

Bo   I won't.

Beat.

Aicha   And *actually* loads of people wanted to chat to me, so jokes on you actually.

Bo (*quiet*)   Yeah, I bet.

Who wouldn't.

A long painful pause.

They meet each other's eyes.

Aicha   It's OK.

Aicha *smiles at her.*

It is restored.

Beat.

Bo   How was it then?

I wish I'd come.

Aicha   It was alright.

Bit boring you know, not gonna lie.

You didn't actually miss much.

Beat – **Aicha** *doesn't know if she should say but she's burning to tell* **Bo**.

Aicha   You know Elliot Park is actually dating Georgia now.

And apparently they go study room at lunch and have sex on those little fold out chairs.

I don't get it at all. Like she is not jokes.

Do you think her bedroom chat is as dead as her lunch chat?

(*As Georgia.*) I actually went to a CLUB at the weekend and the bouncer didn't even check my ID and I drank VODKA and lime and everybody wanted to have SEX with me and my phone is the newest one you can get.

Bo *laughs.*

It's just bullshit 'cause it's not like I even liked him that much, but then even Billy was saying he reckoned he was into me, so I thought like fuck it, might as well put yourself out there, live once and all that.

And now I'm like was it all just some fucking joke.

Getting the geek to ask Ellyboy out.

And now I bet Georgia thinks she's such a fucking legend.

You know she barely scrapes Cs and she's doing humanities.

Bo   It doesn't matter.

Just do your own thing, you don't have to worry what they think.

Aicha   Mate. Do you think I don't know that.

I'm at Space Club right now.

I just don't want to be the big joke of the day.

Bo   Aicha /

Aicha   / Yes yes yes, I know what you're going to say.

(*Mock* **Bo**.) 'It's not a competition.'

'You shouldn't be upset about a boy.'

'Humanities are difficult in their own way.'

There is a pause, **Aicha** *looks at* **Bo** *pissed off and expectant.*

Bo   In primary school I couldn't read or write.

And I don't mean at the start of primary school, I mean like, for all of primary school.

And it wasn't like I wasn't trying. Because I was TRYING.

But I just couldn't do it.

And in Year 6 we used to have these spelling tests.

And every test they would read out everyone's scores in order of what they got. And I was always last.

And one day after one such spelling disaster I went into the playground feeling less than tip top about myself.

Thinking maybe I'd play a bit of basketball to try forget about it.

So I join the little queue of kids, and when I get to the front Georgia is on the court.

And when I go to walk on, she goes, in front of everyone, 'Er, I'm not going to play with a Year 6 who can't even spell their own name'.

So next time we're in class, and she goes off to get a calculator from this storeroom just off the corridor, I nice and calmly go and get Fester, the class ferret, and I creep up after her. Then once she's inside I slip Fester in with her, turn the light off, and jam the door with a bin.

And then off I go back to class.

And nobody finds them for fucking ages.

And when they do, what I hadn't quite anticipated is that obviously poor Fester is as freaked out as Georgia, and as a result he has bitten the shit out of her. Like all down her legs and on her cheek, and she's wet herself and she's bleeding and they have to take her to hospital to check all the bites aren't infected and that.

There is a long pause.

She never tells people, I guess 'cause it's so embarrassing. But that's why she calls me a psycho and that is why I know for a fact that Georgia is both a cunt and can't even take a ferret.

So I realllyyy wouldn't waste your time being jelly of her.

Beat – **Aicha** *is staring at* **Bo***.*

Then . . .

Aicha   I think that's my favourite story of all time.

Did you not get suspended?

Bo   They never had proof it was me.

Beat.

Aicha   Weren't your parents really freaking out that you couldn't read?

Bo   They never knew.

Aicha *is a bit stunned.*

Bo   Don't look so worried.

I've worked it out now like.

Scene Thirteen

Lights up on the flat.

Bo *pauses outside, listening.*

Then she enters.

Grud *isn't there.*

Bo *stops for a moment, momentarily confused by this.*

She looks around a bit.

Bo   Hello?

Nothing.

Grud?

He isn't there.

She visibly relaxes.

Bo *goes to sit in* **Grud**'s *chair.*

She pulls out a bag of crisps and starts eating them.

She turns the TV on.

It's fun.

Then we start to see her realise.

It's not fun.

Where is he?

What's he up to?

Bo *is starting to panic.*

She gets up and goes out.

Bo   Grud? /

Scene Fourteen

Space Club.

Aicha   / Don't you think I look weirdly amazing today.

Just like very powerful and amazing.

I saw Billy on the bus in this morning and he gave me this look like 'oh damn'.

I think maybe it's because I'm ovulating.

They start getting things out to start work on Kerbal.

Beat.

Oh my god also I need to tell you about this video he was showing me.

She's messaging Billy.

Wait let me ask him for it – it was MAD.

She looks at **Bo**.

Aicha   So basically, him and Elliot were walking back down by the canal, and they said they saw this like, gross man, but like, seriously fucked up.

Hobbling about, all zoned out.

And he's like. FUCKED. Like covered in blood and vomit, and piss all down his legs and that. Face all bashed up.

Like kind of scary, kind of just really gross, man.

Anyway, they were just watching him for a bit or whatever, 'cause he's quite the sight. But then he starts moving off, so they were like fuck it, let's follow him, 'cause like, what is he even doing.

And they film him all walking about all . . .

Aicha *does an impression.*

Sort of drooling and sort of . . . mouldy looking.

Anyway, then after a bit, he kind of clocks on to where he is.

And he starts waving at all the people going by. Like suddenly manically waving.

And people are getting pure freaked out.

And he keeps waving, all like looking straight at people and waving and waving and doing this weird creepy smile and like waving at little babies in prams and all this.

And people are like 'fuck no'.

So after a while he stops. And he looks pure sad.

And he sits there. Until it's like, he doesn't really remember what just happened and then he just . . .

Does the impression again.

Gets into the canal and just lays there. Soaking in the dirty water, with all the gross water going over his mouth and stuff.

She gets her phone out.

Oh my god he's sent it – look look look.

She shows **Bo** *a video on her phone.*

They watch it – **Aicha** *makes a face.*

Imagine.

So disgusting.

So rank.

Bo *is standing completely still.*

Aicha   You alright?

She is completely frozen.

Bo   What did they do?

Aicha   Nothing I don't think.

Bo   They didn't call anyone?

Aicha   Nah, don't think so, just left it.

Like he was alive and everything. And walking about and that.

And wasn't causing no harm.

Bo *is staring at her.*

Aicha   Weird, innit.

Aicha *is looking at* **Bo** *differently.*

Aicha   Are you OK?

Bo   Yeah, fine.

Aicha   Are you sure? You look a bit shook.

Bo   Yeah, honestly. Just weird. Makes me feel weird.

Aicha   Yeah.

Kind of tragic, innit.

Aicha *is watching her.*

Bo   I think I'm gonna go /

Aicha   / You live round there, hey.

Bo   What?

Aicha   Like in that bit by the motorway, I swear that's the way you go back.

Bo   What of it?

Aicha   Nothing.

There is a long pause, visible agitation is building in **Bo***,* **Aicha** *is watching her.*

Aicha   Do you know him?

We see a flicker of the flat.

Then it's gone.

Bo   What?

We hear a noise.

Aicha   That man . . . do you . . .

Is that someone you know?

Suddenly everything collides.

We are simultaneously in the flat and the college.

Grud *is lying on the floor. He is covered in blood. He looks worse than we have ever seen him – he looks like the person* **Aicha** *has just described.*

Aicha *remains in her scene.*

Bo *stands. Motionless. She speaks her next lines as if in both scenes and also neither of them.*

Bo   Oh my god.

Fuck.

Aicha   Bo?

Bo   What?

Grud *is only semi-conscious, his gross dressing gown is coming apart and his naked body is falling out, limbs everywhere.*

He makes a strange noise.

Aicha   Is that . . .

Bo   Fuck.

Ambulance.

Twenty-eight Delamere Terrace.

Aicha   You know if things are going on for you, you should tell me.

Bo   They aren't, so maybe drop it, yeah.

My mobile. Yeah, yes, it's this one.

Aicha   I tell you all my stuff.

Bo   He's bleeding. I think he's hurt himself.

Aicha   And like . . .

Bo   I don't know, it's hard to tell.

Aicha   I wouldn't tell anyone.

Bo   'Cause he. Like he drinks a bit so it's hard to tell.

Aicha   If something was happening . . .

Bo   NOTHING IS HAPPENING.

I'm not gross.

Beat.

Aicha   I didn't say you were gross.

Bo (*mock* **Aicha** *from before*)   'Really gross man.'

'So disgusting.'

'So rank.'

Beat.

Aicha   Yeah, but I didn't mean. . .

Bo   I think he's hurt himself.

He's done it before.

Pause.

Just fuck off, yeah.

The college dissipates, **Aicha** *is gone and we are just in the flat.*

Pause.

Bo   Yeah, it's a relative.

It's my dad.

Blackout.

Scene Fifteen

From now on all places exist together.

Bo *moves into the college.*

It is late at night, dark, quiet.

She finds Kerbal.

She calmly takes out a knife and cuts at each of his wires in turn.

Then she drops him on the floor and she leaves.

Bo *moves back to the flat. She lies in the water of the canal.*

She starts to become rotten.

The canal envelopes her.

Aicha *moves into Space Club. She finds Kerbal.*

She picks him up.

She exits.

Scene Sixteen

Grud *sits in his old shit chair. He looks worse than he has ever done. Cuts and bruises. Surrounding him are piles and piles of cans and rubbish. Enveloping him.*

He is watching bad TV.

Aicha *enters, holding the broken Kerbal.*

She stops a distance away from him.

Aicha   Hi.

Your door is wide open, you know.

Beat – they consider each other for a moment.

I'm Aicha.

I'm looking for Bo.

Grud (*slurred*)   Hi.

He says this very carefully . . .

Aicha.

Yes.

Aicha   Do you know me?

Grud   Yes.

Grud *zones out for a moment, he's worse than we've ever seen him.*

Aicha   Is she here?

Beat – **Grud** *realises he doesn't know.*

Grud (*he is slurring so much it's hard to understand*)   I don't know.

Aicha   Do you know where she might be?

There is a pause.

Grud   The canal.

She likes the canal.

Aicha   OK . . . thanks.

Aicha *leaves.*

Grud *zones in and zones out.*

We aren't sure if he thinks **Aicha** *was* **Bo***, we aren't sure if he thinks she's still there.*

Grud   I'm sorry.

Beat.

I'm sorry I'm sorry I'm sorry.

Scene Seventeen

Bo *lies in the canal, collapsed and broken.*

Aicha *enters, holding Kerbal.*

She stands over **Bo***.*

They look at each other.

Aicha   You broke him.

Bo *doesn't acknowledge her, it's not clear if she's heard or not.*

Aicha   Listen, you can do this if you want.

But you have to fix him first.

She leaves.

There is a pause.

Then **Bo** *crawls out of the water and into the college room.*

Scene Eighteen

Bo *sits. Wet and gross in the college room.*

Aicha *sits opposite.*

They look at each other across Kerbal.

There is a long pause.

Aicha   Sorry for just coming round like that.

Bo   No, it's . . . cool.

An awkward pause.

Aicha   Have you always lived there?

Bo   Yeah.

Aicha   Where's your mum?

Bo   I don't know.

It's always just been me and Grud.

Pause.

But like, I get that he probably didn't give birth to me.

Aicha *laughs slightly at this.*

They start to ease tentatively back into their familiarity.

Aicha   Is that his name?

Bo   Nah. It's a nickname.

She's embarrassed.

It's his 'monster name'.

Just a stupid old joke.

Pause.

Aicha (*as if learning the name*)   Grud.

Bo *smiles a bit.*

Bo   It's weird when you say it.

Beat.

Aicha   Come on then.

Aicha *gestures to Kerbal.*

They begin to work on him together.

Standing closer and closer together as they go.

Pause.

Bo   I'm really sorry I broke him.

Bo *is starting to get really upset.*

Aicha   It's all good.

Bo *is starting to panic, she's trying to suppress it but it's not working.*

Aicha *clocks her.*

Aicha   Whoahhhh, oh my god, calm down.

It's just Kerbal, mate, we'll get him fixed.

Bo   I don't know if you should be around me.

Aicha   What?

Bo   I'm serious.

There are really bad things inside of me, Aicha.

Aicha   No there isn't.

Bo   And I'm just pretending really well, but under there I'm made from something rotten and gross.

Deep down at my core.

And I'll do bad things.

I know it. Because I think them. All the time.

I think really fucked up things.

And one day I am going to do them.

Because that's what people like me do, isn't it.

We do bad and fucked up things.

And I've never loved anyone like how I love you.

And I think maybe I can't do it.

There is a long pause.

Aicha   You aren't going to do bad things, you twat.

Bo   You don't know that.

Aicha   I do actually.

I'm your mate, I know what you're like.

And you aren't pretending, you dickhead.

You're just doing it.

Pause.

You're going to go to uni and make pals and eat pasta and have sex and drink too much and be embarrassing and graduate and get shit jobs and get better jobs, and learn to cook and feel lost, and regret things, and feel proud, and rent rooms and fuck up tax bills and fall in love and fall out of it and eat sandwiches and go to parties and go on little holidays and get promotions and get told off, and fuck things up and get things right and have arguments and live in shit flats, and live in cute flats and have a cute baby and teach it how to be a legend, just like how you're a legend. And you're going to do all of it and you're going to be happy. And I'm going to do it with you.

And that's what's going to happen now, OK?

Bo *is crying.*

Bo   I don't think I can leave him.

Aicha   You can.

Bo   I think he'll die.

Beat.

Aicha   Then he wants to die.

There is a long pause.

I'm going to put the projector on.

Bo   OK.

You better not be planning a speech about how all my problems are small and insignificant in comparison to the vastness of space.

Aicha *smiles.*

Aicha   I wasn't going to say that.

I think in comparison to space you are very huge and important.

Aicha *puts the projector on.*

They watch it for a bit.

Aicha *holds* **Bo***'s hand.*

Scene Nineteen

Grud *sits in the semi-darkness, barely moving.*

Bo *stands.*

She is calm and controlled.

Bo   Listen.

I'm sorry you're sad, OK.

I'm sorry about what happened to you to make you so sad.

But I'm not staying here with you anymore.

I'm going to go out there, and I'm going to have a go.

And I think you should too.

There is a pause.

Bo *leaves.*

Grud *closes his eyes with the pain of it, he remains like this, we watch him for a while.*

Scene Twenty

Manchester.

Things are bright and clear.

For the first time we cannot feel **Grud**'s *presence.*

Bo *and* **Aicha** *enter,* **Bo** *is holding Kerbal.*

You can tell immediately they've had an excellent day.

Bo (*mock outrage*)   AICHA.

Aicha *grins at her.*

Bo   You lying bastard.

Aicha *begins to crack up.*

Aicha   It was fun!

And they don't do space launches from the UK, you should really know that actually.

Bo *is giving her a mock angry look.*

Bo   Literally so pointless.

Aicha   Pointless!

POINTLESS?!

An *exclusive* tour of the Hubble telescope.

A *magical* once in a lifetime experience watching the US space launch live streamed at the University of Manchester, surrounded by the researchers whose own CubeStat was on board.

Wouldn't call that pointless, mate.

Besides, we wouldn't have got the atmosphere if we'd just watched it by ourselves, would we.

Nice to do it with a crew.

Eating all the little space-themed snacks.

Good for the vibes.

Beat.

They look at each other.

Both of them crack up.

Bo   This project is SO SHIT.

Aicha   Ahhh.

Yeah.

She laughs.

Was a jokes day, tho!

Bo   Yeah, it was pretty fun.

Aicha   And it does make you kinda hyped for uni, doesn't it?

Bet it's all like mad space launches and then nights out using lasers to set fire to shots before you down them!

Or whatever they'll do on maths.

They look at each other, suddenly realising that isn't with each other.

Aicha   And London and Sheffield are super close, so like we'll be visiting each other all the time.

Bo   Yeah. Yeah, for sure.

Beat.

Aicha   Hang on, wait there, I've got something to show you.

Aicha *exits.*

Bo *stands, looking confused.*

After a moment **Aicha** *returns holding a massive bunch of balloons.*

She stands, holding them. Grinning.

Bo   Who are they for?

Aicha   Errrrr, our main man.

The big dog.

Beat.

Big K.

Bo   I don't follow.

Aicha   He's getting his own bloody launch, isn't he.

Bo   Oh my god, no.

Aicha *grins.*

Bo   I don't know if they'll carry him, he's deceptively heavy.

Aicha   They will, they will.

Give him here.

Bo *passes over Kerbal.*

Aicha *begins to attach the balloons to him.*

Bo *watches her.*

Bo   Aicha, this is quite cringe.

Aicha   –

Bo   What's he even going to look for, to see if there's water in Stockport?

Aicha   Shut up.

Aicha *continues to prepare Kerbal for his lift off.*

Bo   Poor Kerbal, having to watch real Kerbal go off into space and then just getting a balloon ride.

Aicha   Everyone's journey is exciting and valuable and unique.

As she prepares Kerbal, **Aicha** *does an enthusiastic pretend American space launch.*

'Oxygen and helium currently being loaded, completion at T-minus 2 minutes.'

She makes the noise of oxygen and helium being loaded.

'The oxygen is fully loaded. I repeat fully loaded.'

'Bo, could we have confirmation that you are ready?'

Bo *looks at her.*

Aicha   Bo, could we please have confirmation that you are ready?

Bo   I'm ready.

Aicha (*to Kerbal*)   Kerbal, could we please have confirmation that you are ready?

(*Being Kerbal, deep powerful voice.*) 'I am ready.'

'Then we.'

'Have.'

'LIFTOFF.'

Aicha *makes the noise of rockets firing as she lets go of Kerbal.*

They watch him rise into the sky.

Aicha   Goodbye, Kerbal!

Good luck on your big mission.

God.

You know I'm really going to miss that guy.

Kerbal is gone.

Bo   Aicha.

Aicha   Yeah?

Bo   Thank you.

Aicha   For what?

Bo   I think you saved my life.

Aicha   Ah, it's no biggie.

Would have done it for anyone.

Bo *laughs.*

Bo   Dickhead.

Scene Twenty-One

Some time has passed.

There is no college and flat now. There is only one place.

Bo *is older. Carrying herself differently.*

She stands, waiting. Watching the entrance.

After a moment a man appears.

He looks normal, unthreatening, almost fatherly.

It is **Grud**.

They look at each other.

There is a long pause.

Bo   Hello.

Beat.

Grud   Hello.

Blackout.

End.

Methuen Drama Modern Plays

include

Bola Agbaje
Edward Albee
Ayad Akhtar
Jean Anouilh
John Arden
Peter Barnes
Sebastian Barry
Clare Barron
Alistair Beaton
Brendan Behan
Edward Bond
William Boyd
Bertolt Brecht
Howard Brenton
Amelia Bullmore
Anthony Burgess
Leo Butler
Jim Cartwright
Lolita Chakrabarti
Caryl Churchill
Lucinda Coxon
Tim Crouch
Shelagh Delaney
Ishy Din
Claire Dowie
David Edgar
David Eldridge
Dario Fo
Michael Frayn
John Godber
James Graham
David Greig
John Guare
Lauren Gunderson
Peter Handke
David Harrower
Jonathan Harvey
Robert Holman
David Ireland
Sarah Kane

Barrie Keeffe
Jasmine Lee-Jones
Anders Lustgarten
Duncan Macmillan
David Mamet
Patrick Marber
Martin McDonagh
Arthur Miller
Alistair McDowall
Tom Murphy
Phyllis Nagy
Anthony Neilson
Peter Nichols
Ben Okri
Joe Orton
Vinay Patel
Joe Penhall
Luigi Pirandello
Stephen Poliakoff
Lucy Prebble
Peter Quilter
Mark Ravenhill
Philip Ridley
Willy Russell
Jackie Sibblies Drury
Sam Shepard
Martin Sherman
Chris Shinn
Wole Soyinka
Simon Stephens
Kae Tempest
Anne Washburn
Laura Wade
Theatre Workshop
Timberlake Wertenbaker
Roy Williams
Snoo Wilson
Frances Ya-Chu Cowhig
Benjamin Zephaniah

Methuen Drama Contemporary Dramatists

include

John Arden (two volumes)
Arden & D'Arcy
Peter Barnes (three volumes)
Sebastian Barry
Mike Bartlett
Clare Barron
Brad Birch
Dermot Bolger
Edward Bond (ten volumes)
Howard Brenton (two volumes)
Leo Butler (two volumes)
Richard Cameron
Jim Cartwright
Caryl Churchill (two volumes)
Complicite
Sarah Daniels (two volumes)
Nick Darke
David Edgar (three volumes)
David Eldridge (two volumes)
Ben Elton
Per Olov Enquist
Dario Fo (two volumes)
Michael Frayn (four volumes)
John Godber (four volumes)
Paul Godfrey
James Graham (two volumes)
David Greig
John Guare
Lee Hall (two volumes)
Katori Hall
Peter Handke
Jonathan Harvey (two volumes)
Iain Heggie
Israel Horovitz
Declan Hughes
Terry Johnson (three volumes)
Sarah Kane
Barrie Keeffe
Bernard-Marie Koltès (two volumes)
Franz Xaver Kroetz
Kwame Kwei-Armah
David Lan
Bryony Lavery
Deborah Levy
Doug Lucie

Alistair MacDowall
Sabrina Mahfouz
David Mamet (six volumes)
Patrick Marber
Martin McDonagh
Duncan McLean
David Mercer (two volumes)
Anthony Minghella (two volumes)
Rory Mullarkey
Tom Murphy (six volumes)
Phyllis Nagy
Anthony Neilson (three volumes)
Peter Nichol (two volumes)
Philip Osment
Gary Owen
Louise Page
Stewart Parker (two volumes)
Joe Penhall (two volumes)
Stephen Poliakoff (three volumes)
David Rabe (two volumes)
Mark Ravenhill (three volumes)
Christina Reid
Philip Ridley (two volumes)
Willy Russell
Eric-Emmanuel Schmitt
Ntozake Shange
Sam Shepard (two volumes)
Martin Sherman (two volumes)
Christopher Shinn (two volumes)
Joshua Sobel
Wole Soyinka (two volumes)
Simon Stephens (five volumes)
Shelagh Stephenson
David Storey (three volumes)
C. P. Taylor
Sue Townsend
Judy Upton (two volumes)
Michel Vinaver (two volumes)
Arnold Wesker (two volumes)
Peter Whelan
Michael Wilcox
Roy Williams (four volumes)
David Williamson
Snoo Wilson (two volumes)
David Wood (two volumes)
Victoria Wood

For a complete listing of
Methuen Drama titles, visit:
www.bloomsbury.com/drama

Follow us on Twitter and keep up to date
with our news and publications
@MethuenDrama